I0471109

The iCorporation

How to Use Your Own Corporation to
Save Taxes,
Gain Privacy,
Protect Your Assets
and
Raise Money

Dean Willeford

© 2013-2014
by **Dean Willeford**

All Rights Reserved. No part of this publication may be reproduced in any form or by any means, including scanning, photocopying, or otherwise without prior written permission of the copyright holder.

First Printing, 2013, second edition 2014

Printed in the United States of America

ISBN 13:978-1489580566

Income Disclaimer

This document contains business strategies, marketing methods and other business advice that, regardless of my own results and experience, may not produce the same results (or any results) for you. I make absolutely no guarantee, expressed or implied, that by following the advice below you will make any money or improve current profits, as there are several factors and variables that come into play regarding any given business.

Primarily, results will depend on the nature of the product or business model, the conditions of the marketplace, the experience of the individual, and situations and elements that are beyond your control.

As with any business endeavor, you assume all risk related to investment and money based on your own discretion and at your own potential expense.

Liability Disclaimer

By reading this document, you assume all risks associated with using the advice given below, with a full understanding that you, solely, are responsible for anything that may occur as a result of putting this information into action in any way, and regardless of your interpretation of the advice.

You further agree that our company cannot be held responsible in any way for the success or failure of your business as a result of the information presented below. It is your responsibility to conduct your own due diligence regarding the safe and successful operation of your business if you intend to apply any of our information in any way to your business operations.

Terms of Use

You are given a non-transferable, "personal use" license to this product. You cannot distribute it or share it with other individuals.

Also, there are no resale rights or private label rights granted when purchasing this document. In other words, it's for your own personal use only.

The
ICorporation

How to Use Your Own Corporation to
Save Taxes,
Gain Privacy,
Protect Your Assets
and
Raise Money

About the Author

For over 25 years author, consultant and speaker Dean Willeford has specialized in helping small businesses and entrepreneurs start, grow and protect their businesses. He is the principal of BDS Consulting Group and author of <u>CASH OUT</u>, a guide for corporation owners to take money out of their corporation with out disastrous tax consequences. He is a RTRP with the IRS and has prepared thousands of tax returns for corporations, LLCs, partnerships and individuals.

He is available for speaking engagements and consulting assignments.

If you are serious about improving your business' bottom line and would like to schedule a free consultation to see how Dean can help you start a business, or help your businesss grow and prosper, contact him at <u>BDSConsult@gmail.com</u> or call 775- 827-1775.

Thank you for buying our book.

Please **Review** this book on Amazon.com.

We need your feed back to make the next version better.

We want to hear from you. As the reader of this book, you are our most important commentators. We value your feedback.

You can email or write to let us know what you did or didn't like about the book. We would like to know what other areas you would like to see us publish on.

When you contact us, please be sure to include the book's title as well as your name and e mail address.

E mail: Corporatepublishing@msn.com

Mail: Wall Publishing, Corp.

Att: Reader Feedback

3680 Grant Drive, Suite N

Reno, NV 89509

Contents

> **Medical Reimbusement Plans, Retirement plans, Hire Your Children, Educational Assistance Plans, Insurance, Vehicle, Travel and 20 other tax savings.**

Introduction
Definitions and Explanations

The primary purpose of this book is to highlight the amazing benefits of incorporating your business. It is a basic primer and "eye opener" about the corporate form.

Is the government taking too much of your hard earned money? Are you worried about people taking away a life time accumulation of your assets? Do you need more money to grow or expand your business? The book will show you how a corporation can solve these problems.

The corporate form is a wonderful invention that has proven durable and useful for over 400 years. It was invented to spread the risk and share the wealth among entrepreneurial people for a common cause.

This book introduces you to the special concept of the iCorporation. An iCorporation is identical to a regular corporation. It has the same legal structure, obligations, privileges, benefits and advantages. However, it is designed specifically for your personal needs- hence the "i" in iCorporation.

The chief difference of an iCorporation is the focus or emphasis it places on the benefits it offers you, or your family ownership. Although, like all corporations, an iCorporation is a separate legal person from its stockholders, the iCorporation is personalized. The iCorporation when designed, customized, and structured properly, bestows great personal benefits on its tightly held ownership of employee/officer/stockholders. It can give you greater legal protection, confidentiality, and tax savings than other forms of business.

For over 25 years the author has been guiding entrepreneurs to open and grow restaurants, pharmacies, retail shops, automotive shops, service businesses, salons, contractors, manufacturers, movers and many others.

After reading the book I promise you will have a much greater understanding and appreciation of a small, wholly owned iCorporation. You will immediately have more money to spend or invest, instead of sending it to some government agency. You will have greater security and privacy when conducting your business.

Every day you wait to take the first step in creating an iCorporation will cost you money and put you at greater risk. Within one week of forming an iCorporation you will begin gaining benefits through your corporation.

This book is aimed at small entrepreneurs and micro businesses with less than $3,000,000 in revenues. Those currently in business or starting a new business venture, who are looking for asset protection, privacy, money generating methods and tax advantages will find the ideas contained herein useful. It is aimed at the entrepreneur and the small business person. It is not intended for the attorney, CPA or Certified Financial Planner who tend to focus on the details and not on the simple message of the book- *There are many greatly underutilized benefits of incorporating your business.*

The reader will certainly not be able to take advantage of every benefit described in this book because of their particular circumstances (age of your children, for example), but there are so many advantages everyone can benefit to a significant extent. The summary of dollar benefits as stated range from $30,000 to over $80,000 per year. The other benefits are not necessarily monetary advantages, but may be in the form of protection, confidentially, the ability to raise money, or estate planning.

Although unconventional, the word Corporation is capitalized. The author wants to continually emphasize the separation of the Corporation from the owners, directors, and officers. This concept is the essence of corporate life. It is the single most important characteristic that brings all the benefits of privacy, tax savings, and protection to its operators. The words, corporation and company, are used interchangeably, even though the author recognizes companies can be partnerships, sole proprietorships, limited liability companies, or limited partnerships.

When you implement any business strategy be sure to have a sound legitimate business purpose, not just to avoid taxes. You must completely document the actions and purpose of your decisions in resolutions to the company's minutes. Finally, be sure to take all the actions to put those decisions in place. For example, secure the required permits, licenses, contracts and documents.

It is easy to incorporate. A simple one page form and the state fees is all it takes. Anyone can do it in ten minutes. No business is too small to gain advantages. Almost every business should incorporate, especially those that interact with the public. Predators and opportunists can take everything you own. You may choose to have a Corporation just for the purpose of holding assets or property outside your name.

The real story is what happens after you receive the approved Articles of Incorporation and corporate Charter back from the state. You need to make decisions about:

- How do I structure my corporation?

- Do you leave it as a regular C corporation or elect to have a S corporation status? And what are the questions to ask to determine the choice.
- How do I get a Federal ID number?
- What benefits can I get from the corporation and how do I implement those benefits?
- Who are your directors and officers and why and how are they selected?
- What do you put into your first meeting minutes of your directors?
- How do you capitalize the new corporation?
- What resolutions do you put into your corporate minutes?
- What kind of stock do you issue? How many shares? Where you do get stock certificates?

My office offers a two page questionnaire to help you make the above decisions before your begin the incorporating process. You can request the questionnaire at BDSConsult@gmail.com.

Many of the subjects this book highlights require good professional help to set up and document. Some strategies are simple, like setting up a Medical Reimbursement Plan. Others demand specialized legal help, like raising money from the public. In either case, you should discuss the techniques with the appropriate professional advisor and customize them to your individual needs.

This book was created to educate and provide some ideas about the advantages of the corporate form. However, laws do vary among the states and are constantly changing. Factual situations are different, and call for specifically designed strategies. It is not within the scope of the book to describe the detailed and intricate legal ramifications of operating a Corporation.

Always seek your own counsel and advice for your

individual circumstances.

The author believes the facts presented here are accurate at the time written, however, neither the author nor the publisher assume any responsibility for any errors. The author and publisher disclaim any liability resulting from the use of any strategies or use of the information contained in the book. The information is not intended as accounting or legal advice.

We welcome your inquiries about any of the subjects addressed in this book. Contact us at BDSConsult@gmail.com.

So, turn the page and get your pencil and note pad out to start saving money, protecting your assets, gain more privacy and generate more money in the next 24 hours.

Chapter 1

What is a Corporation?

Corporations have been around for hundreds of years. . The first modern recognized corporation was Stora Kopparberg, a Swedish mining company in 1347. The corporate form began to be widely used in the 1500 and 1600's to spread the risk of loss among several people, stockholders, that was inherent in shipping and trade. One of the most famous was the Dutch East India Company chartered in 1600. Most people think of corporations as big companies like Wal-Mart, IBM, Microsoft or Apple Computer. These companies are large, well known, international corporations, but the vast majority of corporations are small and owned by a very few individuals, usually less than 10 people.

Let's look at the legal definition of a regular Corporation to see why it was such a valuable invention.

A Corporation is an artificial person or legal person created under the authority of the laws of a state, ordinarily consisting of an association of several individuals, and having a distinct existence from its members, stockholders and officers. It has its own unique name. It is vested with the capacity to exist indefinitely, and act on the powers that its own members give it as a single unit in the matters relating to the common purpose of their association within the powers conferred on it by the state.

So in the eyes of the law the Corporation is a *separate legal person* that has rights and responsibilities under the state law in which it was formed. The Corporation is a distinct and separate entity from the owners. This is the most important aspect of a corporation. It has the same powers as an individual: it can borrow or lend money, own property, conduct business, can sue or be sued, enter into contracts, and can be dissolved.

Always remember-**You are not the Corporation and the Corporation is not You.**

It is sometimes difficult for owners of small corporations to remember that they are separate. It is of the utmost importance that the owners of the Corporation maintain that separation. This is what limits the risk to the stockholder/owner. The stockholder's risk is limited to whatever they put into the Corporation. None of the stockholder's assets outside of the Corporation is at risk.

The owners of the Corporation, stockholders, agreed to make up their own set of rights, duties and responsibilities, usually called Bylaws. The Bylaws are the operating manual for the Corporation. Whatever the stockholders agree on in the Bylaws are its powers, subject to the laws of the state. The decisions and actions of the Corporation are written down in the minutes of the meetings of stockholders and directors. Stockholders elect directors to oversee the officers who carry out those decisions and actions. The directors and officers may be the same people as the shareholders. In some states the shareholders, directors, and officers may be a single person.

The iCorporation is a special version of a regular corporation where the owner is an individual or family that is taking legal advantage of corporate law to reap the most benefits from the corporate form.

Chapter 2

Why Incorporate?

There are four big benefits to incorporating your business. They are:

1. Protect your personal assets.
2. Privacy of your financial affairs.
3. Save tax money.
4. Raising money for your business venture.

Protection. Since a corporation is a separate legal person from its owners, you have the opportunity to legally isolate your personal assets from the business, but still maintain control of the corporation's actions, activities, and assets.

Privacy. A corporation offers the advantage of anonymity if you want. You do not have to appear on any public documents if you choose. The officers, directors and even the stockholders can be other people, but you can still control the corporation by indirect ownership.

Save Tax Money. Tax laws allow for numerous benefits to be paid in several forms to owner/employees. All the benefits can be paid for in pre-tax money. Congress has written tax laws to encourage certain corporate activity. If you don't take advantage of the benefits and the money saved, it would go to pay taxes instead.

Raising Money. A corporation is the perfect form to raise money for projects and expansion. It allows investors to invest as little or as much as they deem prudent. It could spread the investment risk among many people.

Although Corporations can give you all of the above advantages, you should structure your Corporation to achieve your *primary* objective.

For example, if your primary objective is to have privacy, you can structure it to be passive, have a lower number of transactions and have nominee directors and officers. The stock might even be owned by another entity or offshore Corporation. These steps are taken to keep your name off the public record and out of harm's way.

If your Corporation is going to be a full on operating company dealing with the public, having many suppliers and vendors, or is involved in high-risk activities like contracting, restaurant operations or vehicle operations, or manufacturing dynamite you will build it differently. Perhaps it should have fewer assets, or assets that are encumbered by friendly loans or mortgages. The iCorporation may want to take other steps to reduce risks.

In the following chapters we will look at the specific things you can do to reap your benefits.

Chapter 3

Protect Your Personal Assets

Starting and operating a business is extremely difficult. Well over 90% of businesses startups do not succeed to the five-year mark. In some industries, such as the restaurant business, the mortality rate is even higher. There are a number of reasons for such high failure rates, but that is not within the scope of this book. However, there is one that is always looming in the background.

If you are in business you **will** be sued. Even if you're not in business, the chances of a lawsuit are extraordinarily high in America today.

There are over 1.1 million attorneys in America and they need something to do. Legal statistics show that your chances of being sued in any one year are about one in

29

four. There were over 4,000,000 lawsuits filed in the United States in 2011.

Even if you win your lawsuit it can be devastating. Just to prove you're in the right, it can easily cost $25,000-$100,000 to defend an unjust claim. The costs come from attorney fees, depositions, travel, and your time away from work, just to name a few. The psychological cost can be just as severe. Families can be torn apart, the business suffers from neglect, many times your health is affected, and marriages are destroyed. The loss of assets or properties is inevitable to some extent.

You need to separate your business activities and assets from your personal assets, and/or make them extraordinarily difficult or impossible to find.

Negligence lawsuits. Your employees can get your company in big trouble. For example, a food worker could improperly prepare food and get a customer sick. Insurance may or may not cover the risk. But, because they work for you, you will be responsible.

Traffic accidents. Your delivery driver or secretary could hit another car. Because they are on a business errand for you, you will be on the hook. It happens every day. This is the reason some taxi cab companies place each cab in a separate legal entity. They want to separate each cab from the rest of the corporate assets.

Employee and sexual harassment suits. You can be the target of disgruntled employees for dozens of perceived grievances. Unfortunately, the courts are favorably disposed to these complaints.

I recently had a client that was sued for racial discrimination. The Latin employee claimed he was racially harassed and discriminated against (this employee was actually fired for stealing). He had worked there for six years and the employer had five other Latin employees. Still, a lawyer took the case and demanded $50,000 in settlement. My client clearly was not discriminatory in any way. He eventually settled for $8,000, but the total cost to defend himself was $15,000. If he had gone forward with his defence, it would have easily cost more than twice that amount.

If you think these are highly unlikely, consider these surprise jury verdicts against small business owners.

Kathleen Robertson of Austin, Texas was awarded $80,000 after breaking her ankle tripping over a toddle who was running inside a furniture store where she was shopping. The running, out of control toddle was her own son.

Amber C. of Lancaster, a Pennsylvania woman was awarded $113,500 after she slipped on a spilled soft drink at a restaurant and broke her tailbone. The reason the soft drink was on the floor: Ms. C had thrown it at her boyfriend 30 seconds earlier during an argument.

Mrs. Grazinski of Oklahoma City purchased a 32 foot Winnebago motor home. She was driving it to a football game on the freeway and set the cruise control to 70 miles per hour. She calmly left the driver's seat to go to the back to make herself a sandwich. Not surprisingly, the motor home left the freeway and crashed. Mrs. Grazinski sued Winnebago for not putting in the owners manual that she should not leave the driver's seat while the cruise control was set and the vehicle was moving at 70 miles per hour. The jury awarded her $1,750,000 plus a new motor home. Winnabago changed the owner's manual.

You too could become a victim of a court gone wild.

Malpractice suits. Insurance may cover much of the costs associated with these suits, but the deductible that professionals pay can be $50,000 or more. Sometimes insurance does not cover a judgment. Even if you win, your insurance premiums are sure to increase.

Loan guarantees. If you sign a loan agreement to backstop the credit for others, or for your own business, and the loan defaults, the lender can come after you personally.

Business failures. When business goes bad, partners, friends, ex-wives or backers become your worst enemy. They may try to recover their investments, seek a larger part of the business, or try to take control. You will want to have you personal assets protected in this event.

Environmental suits. Federal and state governments are almost impossible to fight, because they have unlimited resources. Penalties and fines can run into millions of dollars. Governmental agencies are famous for seizing your funds, many times without even charging you with a crime. It is up to you to prove your innocence; all the while they hold your assets. The Patriot Act and similar legislation provides for civil asset forfeiture and seizure even if you are even slightly or coincidently related to an alleged crime.

The government has even used the Environmental Protection Agency (EPA) and the IRS to attack businesses for political reasons. In 2011 a major guitar manufacturer was attacked by these federal agencies because the owner was major conservative monetary supporter. After spending millions of dollars to defense itself, all charges were dropped.

There are other non business related threats that can rob you of a life time of accumulated assets.

Medical expenses. Many times unforeseen medical bills can exceed medical insurance coverage. It is easy for catastrophic medical bills to exceed $ 1 million.

Taxes. Large assessment audits may leave you unable to pay. Most taxes are not dischargeable in bankruptcy. Late filing penalties, late payment penalties, interest and negligent filing penalties can easily double a tax bill. The state usually piles on after the IRS is done. Wouldn't it be better if your assets are beyond the reach or knowledge of the taxing authority?

Divorce. Hollywood and business is rife with numerous examples of everlasting love that has burnt out. Even with prenuptial agreements it is best to have a separate financial cushion that only you know about.

You see these nightmare stories every day in the news.

You will want to have your corporate protective shield in place **before** incidents rear their ugly heads. In almost all states the Uniform Fraudulent Conveyance Act prohibits you from selling or transferring assets to avoid legitimate claims *after* the problem.

The best defense is to have little for the lawyers to go after, or make it difficult or impossible to find. You may even have your assets outside of the jurisdiction of the courts in a foreign country. It is not illegal to have an overseas corporation; you just need to disclose foreign accounts of over $10,000 to the IRS.

Separation is Protection

The most important word in the corporate definition is separation. Owners of the iCorporation are not liable for the corporation's debt making the iCorporation one of the best ways to protect your personal assets.

The iCorporation is *not* you, and you are *not* the iCorporation. The iCorporation is a separate legal "person".

When someone sues your iCorporation it does not mean they will not attempt to also sue you personally, but it makes it much more difficult for the court to include you for the alleged wrong doing of the iCorporation. Even if they win, the only thing you have at risk is what you have invested in the iCorporation. They could take the assets of the iCorporation, but in most cases the liquidating value is worth much less than what is shown on the books.

You should have your personal assets outside the iCorporation or owned by some other entity.

Corporate Vail

 Even though a Corporation is designed to protect your personal assets from creditors, one of the first things an attorney for the creditor will try to do is, "pierce the corporate veil". This means that the creditor will attempt to disregard the legal protections afforded by an iCorporation and hold the shareholders, officers, and directors personally liable for the claim.

It is vitally important for the owners, directors and officers to understand the concept of piercing the corporate veil, and to take steps to avoid having the corporate protection discarded. The following is a list of common activities that lend cause to penetrate corporate protection.

An astounding 76% of small corporations run afoul of one of these simple steps. That is why attorneys use these excuses to sue. These steps are easy to comply with.

The concept of "piercing the corporate veil" is based on the legal doctrine of Alter Ego. A corporation used by an individual to conduct *personal* business is not permitted if it would result in fraud or injustice. In short, an individual cannot use a corporation to hide behind if you and the corporation cannot be separated.

Commingling Funds and Assets.

Because owners of small corporations are so closely related to the iCorporation's activities and invested funds, they sometimes feel that they can use the iCorporation's funds or assets for their own use. There is a tendency for owners to use and replace corporate funds as needed or seen fit. Sometimes finances get tight, and it is easy for a corporate owners to write a corporate check for his personal use. They justify using corporate funds since the company *belongs* to them.

Remember the iCorporation is a separate legal entity. You cannot use corporate funds for personal use without consequences. To look at this in other context, let's say the president, director or stockholder of Wal-Mart, Inc. took $100,000 out of Wal-Mart's bank account for their personal use. Everyone would consider that theft. And it is no less true for a small Corporation.The law looks at it in the same way.

Even if the money is paid back, there is an exchange of money without regard to the formal separation between the stockholder and the iCorporation. The creditor could claim that because the iCorporation did not maintain its distinct and separate identity. There really was no separation between the stockholder and the iCorporation. They are one in the same, an Alter Ego.

The iCorporation and you must have separate corporate bank accounts, federal tax identification number, a separate unique name and tax returns.

Another case of co-mingling is the use of corporate assets for both personal and corporate use. For example, you may have a small iCorporation in which you work out of your home, or use your corporate car for personal business. You should have documentation in the corporate minutes to approve and compensate the iCorporation for the personal use of those assets. For example, the Corporation might pay you rent for the use of your home. You should submit an expense report showing the personal use of the company automobile, and compensate the company for that use.

So as you can see, it is of paramount importance to avoid commingling funds between the iCorporation and its owners, directors and stockholders.

There are numerous ways for stockholders to legally take money out of an iCorporation and still maintain the separation. The employee/stockholders can take salaries, dividends, loans, expense accounts, retirement accounts and other compensation. We will cover many of those legal ways to take money out of the iCorporation in Chapter 5. All the methods are beyond the scope of this book, but they need to be properly documented to avoid the comingling issue.

Fraud or Criminal Activity

Another way to pierce the corporate veil is to claim fraudulent or illegal activities on your part. For example, if you used false information on a corporate loan application, you could be held personally liable for the loan repayment, penalties and legal costs.

Don't ever let illegal activity be perpetrated on company property or under the umbrella of the company's name, regardless of how small you think the infraction is.

Corporate Formalities.

An iCorporation must keep records of its decisions. These decisions are usually made at meetings of directors and stockholders. Corporations are required to have at least one meeting per year, although it is quite common to have quarterly or special meetings. At these meetings decisions and actions are discussed and voted on, affirmed and recorded in the minutes of the meeting. Resolutions approved at meetings are what gives the power to the officers to pursue the actions decided on. Decision resolutions are also possible outside of the corporate meeting, if documented properly. These resolutions become the corporate memory.

The formality and the recording of the minutes and resolutions are yet another step to keep the iCorporation separate and distinct from the ownership. If actions and decisions are made without these formal steps it gives a claimant another reason to claim that the owners and the Corporation are one in the same and therefore not separate. A court may set aside the corporate protection if the proper procedures are not followed and open up the officers, directors and shareholders to personal liability.

Our office provides corporate document services to keep your corporate decisions and documents current.

Improperly Signed Documents.

Another common mistake that falls under the heading of corporate formalities is the improper signing of documents by officers. When you sign a document for the iCorporation it is paramount that you follow your signature with your corporate title. This indicates that you are not *personally* signing, but are signing on behalf of the iCorporation. This avoids a situation where a claimant could say that both the corporation and you personally were agreeing to the contract, and therefore could include you in any lawsuit.

I know of a moving and storage company where the owner contracted for more than $50,000 of yellow pages advertising with his signature. The company went bankrupt in a severe recession. Now the yellow pages company is suing the owner for the debt, because they claim he guaranteed the contract *personally*, because he did not use his title when signing for the corporation.

Always make it clear that it is the iCorporation that is doing business with others. Be sure the iCorporation is identified as such with the words Corporation, Inc., Incorporated, Limited, or LTD. This will ensure there is no confusion between you personally and the iCorporation.

The proper signature form is the name of the iCorporation, followed by your name and title. Example

XYZ Corp. Joe Wilson, President

Good Standing

Unfortunately, it is quite common for small corporations to lose their standing with the state of incorporation simply by forgetting to renew their annual filings with the state. If you don't pay your fees, the state will revoke your corporate standing, and you are no longer a legal Corporation, and therefore lose protection of the corporate form. Our company provides a service to keep your iCorporation in good standing.

Taxes.

No matter how tight the funds are, always pay your taxes first. The officers or directors can become liable for those taxes. Absolutely be sure to pay "trust fund" taxes. Trust fund taxes are those the corporation collects for some governmental agency, and then forwards them periodically to the agency. Employee Social Security, federal income withholding taxes and sales taxes are good examples.

The above are common reasons to lose the protection of the corporate veil. It's beyond the scope of this book to get into every possible legal ramification of piercing the corporate veil, but these are important reminders that these details are not nuisances, but are important factors for your protection.

Fraudulent Conveyance

You can't just change the title on assets or create a corporation *after* an event becomes a problem. The law will not allow fraudulent conveyance, which is the transfer of property for little or no consideration, to hinder, delay or place it beyond the reach of creditors. A court can easily reverse the transactions.

Chapter 4

Do You Need Privacy of your

Financial Affairs?

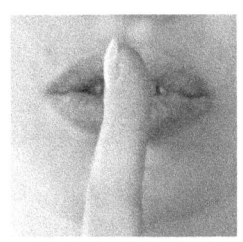 The point of all this conversation about confidentiality has to do with making it more difficult for attorneys, predators, scammers and others who might be after your assets. All those potential liabilities we talked about earlier in Chapter 3 are reasons to keep your financial affairs private.

The best defense against lawsuits is to be totally broke, because if you have nothing, there is no reason for someone to come after you. You can structure your iCorporation to have very little in assets to go after.

A second defense is to be "invisible". Since you can't be totally invisible you want to make your information more difficult to pursue and assets harder to find. Depending on the size of the potential claim, these privacy measures may be enough to discourage a claimant.

If someone takes an interest in you, you are virtually an open book in today's public society. If you have assets that are highly visible you become a target. Using an iCorporation to gain more privacy is about reducing the risk of lawsuits, avoiding scammers, hackers, and other predators.

There is no privacy in America anymore, without taking positive steps to insure it.

With the wide spread use of the Internet, almost anyone can obtain your personal information. Here is a partial list of what is easily available.

Real estate records	Voter registration records
Criminal records	Professional licensing records
Property tax records	Divorce, bankruptcy records
Probate records	Marriage license records
Telephone records	Worker's compensation information
Family information	Utility records

Facebook, Linkedin and other social sites offer almost unlimited personal information.

Governmental agencies have virtually no limits on getting your information. The Patriot Act authorizes the government to obtain financial records without even charging you with a crime.

Currency control regulations require banks to report "suspicious" activities involving deposits or withdrawals of cash. Many banks routinely report cash activities of less than $10,000 and are required by currency control laws to report more than that.

In 2011 Google had over 20,000 requests by governmental agencies to look at email contents of its account holders. In December 2012, it was reported that the National Security Agency records every email of all US citizens via a surveillance device called "Naris". The FBI has access to them. The government does this without your permission. They are building a larger database storage facility in Bluffdale, Utah to house this new facility.

Unfortunately, as shown by recent IRS scandals, the IRS has even shared tax information with outside private orgnizations who have political motivations.

Credit bureaus routinely share your credit information with anyone that has the smallest interest in your financial activities.

In order to get a loan, it is quite common for borrowers to authorize the lender to look at your tax returns, when you sign IRS form 4506T, which is usually included in the loan document package. If you don't authorize the form, they will not consider the loan.

As we mentioned previously, you are not the iCorporation and the iCorporation is not you. Each has a separate identity and separate name. This is the essence of the corporate form to give you liability and asset protection, but it can also lend itself to affording you privacy and confidentiality of much of your financial affairs.

By using an iCorporation, privacy can be achieved at several levels for its owners

The first level of privacy comes from the fact that the iCorporation is separate from you. You can create your iCorporation with a totally separate name that does not suggest your involvement in it at all. Or, you can still be an officer, director or incorporator of the iCorporation and be listed that way in public records. For example, in Nevada the annual filing with the Secretary of State only requires the name and address of the officers and the directors. That means anyone who is interested in your company can go to the internet site of the Nevada Secretary of State's office and see who is listed as the officers and directors. Stockholders are not required to be listed.

A second level of privacy can insulate you when you have other people fill the positions of officers and directors. Those positions could be filled by family members, an attorney or close confidants, although this may suggest to outsiders a possible connection to you. Your ownership is only disclosed in your corporate book, minutes, and stock ledger, which are private.

The third level of confidentiality could be achieved by using nominees, totally unrelated to you, to fill the officers and directors positions. Our company is among a number of companies that provide this service for you. Again, your ownership does not have to be disclosed. The stock of the iCorporation could even be owned by another entity such as another corporation, a partnership, a trust or a limited partnership.

A still deeper level of privacy can be achieved by issuing bearer stock. Nevada is the only state in the union that allows stock to be issued to the bearer with no name on it.

The stock is simply owned by whoever holds it. Your name does not need appear on the company records.

The ultimate secrecy can be achieved by having the officers and directors filled by nominees and the stock would be owned by an offshore corporation. In most cases, the offshore corporation would be out of the jurisdiction of American courts. The records of ownership can be kept offshore also.

The point of this discussion is to illustrate the various levels of privacy that are available depending on your needs. Each level has costs and documentation associated with it.

Chapter 5

How to Save Money and Taxes

There are numerous IRS approved deductions, plans and strategies that can be used to save enormous amounts of money for small iCorporation owner/employees.

Below is a list of benefits that are available to employees, tax-free. They are 100% deductible only by regular C or iCorporations. Some of the benefits can be offered on a discriminatory basis, which means you may pay these benefits to yourself as an employee and not to other employees, if you wish. The nondiscriminatory basic benefits must be offered to all full-time employees, who work more than 1,000 hours per year.

Discriminatory Benefits.

- Disability insurance
- Free parking up $245 per month.
- Annual medical checkups.

- Personal liability insurance, errors insurance for employees, officers and directors.
- $5,000 death benefit. The Corporation may take a deduction for up to $5,000 paid to heirs of any employee.
- Free housing and meals on company premises when employees are required to be there. This must be "for the convenience of the employer". These expenses can be taken at one hundred percent. There must be a written policy stating the conditions.
- Small Christmas gifts. These must fall under the de minimis fringe definition.
- Subscription to business periodicals.
- Payment for professional and business club dues

- Cost of business conventions, including travel, hotels and meals.
- Uniforms, small tools and logo attached protective and safety-related clothing. Cleaning is also included.
- Achievement awards. They must be in-kind personal property, not cash, up to $400 per year.
- Automobile used for business purposes and accountable personal use.

- No interest or low interest loans.

Nondiscriminatory Fringe Benefits.

All of these benefits must be offered to all employees, if offered to any.

- Recreational and health facilities. Must be on premises, operated by the employer.
- Pre-paid legal assistance
- Tuition reimbursement. The iCorporation can provide up to $5,250 per year
- Meal expenses provided to employees tax-free and deductible if provided for occasional and sporadic meal reimbursements and money for meals for overtime work.
- Employee medical expenses reimbursement plan.
- Child and dependent care expenses up to $5,000 a year.
- $50,000 of group term life insurance. Income tax-free, but subject to Social Security taxation.
- $2,000 in group term life for dependence.
- Discounts on company products and services.
- No additional cost services or the services readily offered for sale to customers. An example is free airline employee travel.

- Qualified achievement awards provided under a written plan for longevity or safety. A Corporation may award up to $1,600 per year.
- A corporation is able to deduct up to twice the basis in inventory costs for donations to charity.
- Various kinds of retirement plans are available, each with limits. Pension plans, 401(k), profit sharing, SEP-IRA, SIMPLE- IRA, etc.
- Travel, if carefully planned to take maximum advantage of the IRS rules.
- Educational Reimbursements and Allowances
- Health insurance
- Adoption assistance – up to $12,970.

In this chapter we will focus on just six of the largest fringe benefits that could in total be worth in excess of $80,000 per year. These are ideal for small one person or family owned iCorporations.

They are:

Medical reimbursement plans

Retirement plans

Hiring your children and family members

Insurance

Vehicle use

Education plans

*Travel/entertainment/meals (optional)

Medical Reimbursement Plans.

A medical reimbursement plan could easily be worth $10,000 or more per year.

These plans are so valuable because they allow the iCorporation to pay for your medical expenses and it can write them off as business expenses, thereby lowering the iCorporation's taxes. This type of plan is covered by Internal Revenue Code section 106(e).

The plan can cover both you and your family. The plan can pay a percentage or the total of those medical expenses. Medical plans can have an enormous impact on your tax bill. If you have a large family the amount paid out could be considerable. Also, you do not have to limit the tax deduction on your personal taxes by 10%. For example, if you had an adjusted gross income of $100,000, the first $7,500 of medical expenses would not be deductible on your personal tax return. But the iCorporation has no such limit.

In an iCorporation that has more employees than just close family, it would be advisable to set up a limit to the maximum that the company would pay out. For example, the Plan would reimburse up to $3,000 per year. As an alternative, you could set up a high deductible outside insurance plan and have the Plan pay up to that deductible amount.

You may exclude the following employees from your corporate reimbursement plan:

-employees that have not attained the age of 25

-employees who have not completed three years of service

-part-time or seasonal employees

-employees that are covered by collective bargaining agreement

One of my clients is a pharmacist who has five employees. Two are covered by collective bargaining agreements, one is a part-time employee, and two others are family members who provide legitimate full-time services to the pharmacy. So, he can be quite generous with the Plan' coverage and still have all the benefits for his family.

Medical reimbursement plans are usually simple agreements of one or two pages that outline the benefits, eligibility, the limitations, submission of proof for medical expenses, and definition of who sets the rules. You should call a special meeting of the directors of the iCorporation to put the Plan in place and include that resolution in meeting minutes. A sample Plan is included in the forms section.

Retirement Plans

Although there are several retirement plans available, we will focus on the ones that benefit small owner operator iCorporations the most.

This benefit could be worth as much as $52,000.

Simplified Employee Pension Plans (SEP) are simplified retirement plans that Corporations can set up for employees. Each employee participant has his own individual retirement account to which the employer can contribute. Annual employer contributions are not mandatory, so the employer has more flexibility in determining the amount they contribute, if any. The employer can set up a plan for any year as late as the due date for filing the taxes for that year.

The big advantage of a SEP over a regular IRA is that the contribution limits are much higher. The contributions by the employer can be up to 25% of an employee's compensation or $52,000, whichever is lower. Contributions are made on a percentage basis of each employee's compensation and it must be the same for all employees. So, for a small owner operator family iCorporation, this type of plan might be ideal.

The big disadvantage is that SEPs are nondiscriminatory and therefore, an employer must contribute to the SEP of all participants who are employees, including those who die or terminate before the contributions are made. So, from the employer's perspective, depending on the number of employees, a 401(k) plan or other qualified plans might be more practical.

Since the iCorporation is making the contributions, it becomes an expense that lowers the iCorporation's taxes and becomes a current non-taxable benefit to the owner-employee.

SEPs are my favorite retirement plan because they are inexpensive to set up and there are no complicated annual tax filings as with other qualified plans. The company only has to complete IRS Form 5305-SEP and keep it with the company's internal records.

401k is simply a profit sharing plan that allows the employee to defer their compensation into their retirement years. The iCorporation can contribute up to 25% of an employee's compensation and the employee can defer up to $17,500, (plus the "catch up" of $5,500 for those 50 and older) for a total of $23,000 or less, up to 100% of compensation.

If you and your spouse are the only employees, try this. Set the spouse's salary at $1,400 per month, $16,800 per year. The spouse chooses to defer $16,800. The company gets a $16,800 deduction for the spouse's salary, the iCorporation can deduct $4,200 as its contribution (25% of 16,800), the family gets a $21,000 ($16,800+$4200) investment to set aside and grow. You pay no taxes on your personal income tax return.

You could do more. You can play with numbers since you could go up to a total of $17,500 per employee deferral and the company's 25% of compensation to a maximum of $51,000. For example, if the spouse received $24,000 salary, they could defer $17,500, the company puts in $6,000(25%of $24,000) for a total of $23,500 to invest. The company still deducts $24,000 in salary, and $6,000 in contribution. But in this case, the difference between $24,000 and the deferred ($17,500) is $6,500 which would be taxable on personal taxes. So, you get the maximum advantage in the first scenario.

You have complete flexibility, because the contribution and the deferral are not mandatory.

An additional advantage is that you can borrow from the plan up to 50% of the account balance up to $50,000. You can't do this with a regular IRA Account.

Finally, most qualified retirement plans provide a great deal of legal protection because they are exempt from creditors.

The problem with qualified plans, such as the 401k and profit sharing is they require a lot of paper work and administration.

See a qualified retirement plan specialist for the details of each plan.

Hire Your Children

 One of the simplest ways to save taxes and increase your family income is to hire your children. For every child you hire your corporation can deduct $6,100. and the child pays no income tax on it. You can still take the child as a $3,900 exemption on your personal tax return.

Great care should be taken to document the "child-employee" as a bona fide employee. It is critically important that the iCorporation treat the child as it would any other employee. The minimum age for the child should be six. You should create an employment file with a simple employment application with the basic information about the child "employee". In that file you should have all the documentation as with any other employee,

61

such as a W-4 form, I-9 form, a copy of their driver's license or identification, social security card and even a simple one-page employment contract. The contract should detail their duties and their pay rate. The child employee should complete timecards. They should be paid by company check no more often than weekly, preferably every two weeks or monthly. File the payroll form 941 and any state forms. At year's end the employees must receive a W-2.

You should do a brief survey to see what wages are being paid for comparable work in other companies. Pay your child similar wages for similar types of work in those companies.

And finally, the child employee must do the work to be a bona fide employee.

Even though the company will have to pay the 7.65% Social Security and Medicare tax, which goes into the employees Social Security account, the savings are impressive. The company gets to deduct the $6,100. as legitimate employee wages. At the lowest corporate tax rate of 15%, there is a savings of $870 in corporate income tax, $1,450 at the 25% rate, and $1,972 at the 34%

rate, finally $2,088 at the 36% tax rate.

Another major benefit of this arrangement is that it teaches the child about business and the employee/company relationship. You could have the child employee complete his own timecards, submit them on a timely basis and report to you about the work that they have done. You get to critique their performance and teach valuable work place skills.

Open a bank account for the child employee. Teach the child about the use of a checking or savings account. The employment will teach the child the value of work and the pride of having his own job.

The money that the children earns can be used in any way they like. They can save or spend all or part of it. They can start an educational fund, which with interest over the years, could be considerable. The interest on that account also accumulates tax-free in their name. So, in effect, the Corporation can be paying a large part of the college or technical education costs and gets a deduction for it.

Each child could establish a Roth Individual Retirement Account (ROTH-IRA) in their own name and could contribute up to $5,500 a year. This account could accumulate tax-free for years. The compounding effect can be enormous over the years. At a 5% grow rate and adding contributions each year, for 10 years, the IRA could grow to over $100,000. This amount could pay for a college education, home down payment or to be used to start a business. The money that is contributed can be withdrawn tax free after the initial five year holding period.

A second alternative.

If you'd like to take some these benefits a step further you can pay your child even more.

You can take your child off your personal tax return and forgo the $3,900 exemption.

The child could then take their own $3,900 exemption, plus their $6,100 standard deduction, for a total of $10,000. The child could earn up to $10,000 and still be tax exempt.

The child could also be included in the retirement plan of the corporation. The iCorporation could deduct the retirement contributions and further reduce its own taxes, but also keep more income for the family.

The child, over 21 years of age, now can take advantage of the corporate educational assistance plan up to $5,250 per year.

Make calculation comparisons that consider the age of the child and the current tax rates to determine the greatest tax savings.

This technique can also be used by a sole proprietor and it even saves the Social Security and Medicare taxes of the "employee".

Education Assistance Plan

Under section 127 of the IRS code, a corporation can deduct $5,250 in educational expenses paid to assist employees under a written educational assistance plan. The assistance is not considered compensation to the employee. Tax-free assistance to eligible employees need not be for job related courses. Tuition, fees, books, and equipment are covered, but room and board is not. It must be in a separate written plan and cannot be part of a section 125 Cafeteria Plan. No more than 5% of the benefit can go to stockholders.

Children of owners can qualify if they are over the age of 21, are not dependents of the owners and do legitimate work as employees for the company. Think of some of the possibilities for small corporate owners who have grown children.

Insurance

 Insuring large parts of your life can be expensive, but your iCorporation can pay many of those expenses and not be taxable to you. There are too many variables to reliably estimate the total possible savings that an iCorporation can save you, but it is usually well worth the cost savings to take advantage of the corporate form. The most important aspect of these expenses is that the iCorporation pays them, thus lowering its corporate taxes, yet provides you with a personal benefit. Your iCorporation can pay life insurance, errors and omissions insurance, disability and health/medical insurance, general liability insurance for

your office or business premises and even group life for your spouse and dependents.

Life insurance (IRS Section 79) Your iCorporation can pay the premiums on a group term life insurance policy up to $50,000 on your life. Depending on your age and health, this could easily be worth $500 more in savings per year. You can have more than $50,000 coverage, but you would be taxed on the premium value of the additional coverage. The excess premiums payments would be added to your W-2 income. The company can also provide up to $2,000 on a group term life insurance policy for your dependents.

E &O insurance. Your iCorporation can and should purchase Errors and Omissions insurance to protect you and the iCorporation from unintentional errors or acts of omission. Attorneys, insurance brokers, real estate brokers, and all sorts of other professionals need to have E&O insurance to protect them from lawsuits. The premiums for this type of insurance depend on your record. It can be from a few hundred to several thousand dollars per year.

Health medical and disability coverage. The cost of health insurance has skyrocketed in the last few years and will only continue to climb. In general, gross income of an employee does not include employer provided coverage under an accident or health plan (IRS sec 206(a). Your iCorporation can pay for these.

In fact, the iCorporation will be required to pay for this coverage under the Affordable Care Act(Obama Care)for over 50 employees. The ACT requires plans to offer child coverage up to 26 years of age, unless they have coverage elsewhere. You should structure and coordinate this kind of insurance with your health reimbursement plan mentioned earlier, depending on the number of employees you have.

General liability insurance. Protect yourself and business against liability claims. All businesses should have a business owner's policy. When bundled with coverage for fire, flood, theft and destruction of valuable business papers it is a very affordable business expense.

Employee Death Benefit (IRS section 101)

Any amounts, up to $5,000 received as a death benefit by your family or estate could be excluded from income. Again another deduction for the Corporation and a tax free benefit for your family.

Talk with a good insurance agent to discuss cost and coverage for each of the above.

Dependent Care Assistance

 The corporation could pay up to $5,000 per year for Dependant Care Assistance ($2,500 for married, filing separately). To qualify the children must be under 13 years of age and the spouse must work and have at least $5,000 in earned income. You must provide the iCorporation with the care provider's name, address, and tax identification number. That information must be listed on the personal return.

I hesitate to include it as a big benefit for small owner corporations, because there are severe limits. No more than 25% of the benefits can go to more than 5% or more stockholders or owners. But, this benefit can be valuable for retaining good employees.

The employee must examine the tax provisions on IRS Form 2441 to determine if they would qualify for this benefit or if it might be useful.

Vehicles

 There is a lot of misinformation surrounding company owner automobile use. The general rule for automobile use is that the employee is taxed on the *personal* use portion including commuting. But, a corporation can pay an automobile allowance. This is considered an accountable plan under IRS regulations. It is reportable on your personal income tax, if the reimbursement exceed the mileage rate established by the federal government. Although the standard mileage rate varies from year to year, in 2014 it is $.56 per mile.

Let's say the business use of the automobile averages out to be about 1,000 miles per month. At $.56 per mile, times 1,000 miles, that would equal $560 a month, or $6,720 per year. Although you would pay the insurance, maintenance, oil and gas that should be enough to cover the costs on most automobiles.

The employee would be required to keep good business mileage records to substantiate the business use of the automobile. You should report this business mileage to the company on a regular basis. If you do not prove the business usage to the iCorporation the entire allowance would be considered as a non-accountable plan and would be reported as income on the employee's W-2.

We suggest you keep a mileage record booklet in the car and record the business and personal use miles at the end of each day. This would substantiate the business use. Remember, no substantiation, no deduction. (See Vehicle Usage Log for the required IRS documentation in the Sample section.)

The company can also reimburse you for parking and tolls separate from the above allowance.

The effect of the allowance is that the company is paying for your automobile and you have the option to select the type of automobile that you would like to drive.

The other methods the IRS approves have limits on owner/employees or are only useful for small inexpensive cars, or result in additional personal use income on your W-2.

*Travel, Meals and Entertainment

Some authors like to include travel, entertainment and meals as big benefits. Travel is only a personal benefit if carefully planned to adhere to the numerous IRS rules.

Can you turn a vacation into a tax deductible expense? Yes, if you follow the rules. However the rules are complicated. First, you need to know the IRS definitions concerning travel. Those definitions will determine how much personal benefit you can get out of business travel. Business intent is the key element in determining if travel is business related. Always keep good records of expenses and business meetings. Planning is the key to get any personal benefit.

Business travel is deductible when your business activity requires you to sleep or rest away from your principal place of business. The travel must be conducted with the intent of obtaining a direct business benefit; appropriate and useful to develop and maintain your business; and finally customary and usual within your industry.

It is important to recognize there are two parts to business travel. One is "transportation expense" that gets you *to* the business. Airfare, train and automobile expenses are examples. The other is "business day expenses" you incur while you are *at* the business location. These include lodging, food, rental cars, and other incidental costs. The two kinds of travel expenses are handled differently. 100% of both are deductible, except meals which are 50% deductible. Business travel transportation expenses are accounted for by the number of "business day". A business day is defined as at least four hours plus one minute of business activity.

One of the key concepts of deductible business travel is the 51/49% rule. For the 50 states, you can deduct 100% of the transportation if you spend more than half of your time on business. Weekends, holidays and transit days count as business days when they fall between the normal business days. For example, if you travel Thursday, do business Friday, play golf on Saturday and Sunday, work Monday and return home Tuesday, you have spent 6 days on business. The entire transport costs are deductible, as are the 6 lodging and food days. If you added on 4 days of vacation at the *end* of the stay, the transportation is 100% deductible, but you would not take food and lodging expenses for the final 4 days. If the purpose of the trip is not primarily for business, you lose all transportation deductions. However, if you conduct business on several of those days, your may deduct "day expenses" for those days.

If you travel by car for business transportation be aware that 300 miles plus per day is considered a business day and therefore eligible to take a full day of travel expenses.

Travel on a ship is divided into two different business categories. There is ship transportation travel and educational courses that take place on cruise ships. Take care of promoters that claim cruise seminars are deductible. The maximum amount you can deduct each year is $2000. if you meet four conditions.

- The ship must be U.S. registered.
- All ports of call are in the United States or U.S. possessions.
- More than 50% of your total days should be spent on business. If you only spent one day on business on a five day cruise it would not be deductible.
- In order to get the deduction, when you file your tax return you must submit a statement stating the days of transportation, the number of hours of the trip, and the program of scheduled business activities. Also you will need a statement signed by the official of the company showing the number of

hours of the business seminar and how many hours you attended.

Since the IRS does not specify the mode of travel for your business trip, you could take a slow boat to Europe. Remember all business day expenses are deductible. So, if you take six days to go from New York to London by boat, all the expenses are deductible but limited by a special IRS rule. The deduction cannot exceed twice the highest Federal per diem rate. So, if that rate is $320, your deduction is limited to $3840 ($640x6days). Planning business trips can be very valuable to you.

Travel out of the country has its own set of tax rules. The IRS allows you to deduct transportation expenses of the total trip relative to the total number of business days. If you have a twelve day trip, and eight of those days are deemed business ,66.7% would be deductible(8 divided by 12 days), (Note the above boat trip to Europe are travel day expenses not transportation expenses.)

There are two exceptions to the above for foreign travel that allow you to take 100% of the expenses. One is the "one week" loophole. If you are back home in less than 7 days, regardless of the number of business days, 100% of the transportation expense are deductible(Sec 2033-2036

IRC). Leave Monday to visit a business supplier in Paris for a day, spend the next 4 days sightseeing, and be home by Sunday, transportation is 100% deductible.

The second exception is that you can be gone as long as you like, if your total business days exceed 75% of total days away, 100% of the transportation is deductible.

So, you can see there are lots of opportunities to gain benefits from your business travel. Just make sure it fits into the rules above.

Many business people consider travel a necessary nuisance and not really a personal benefit, so I don't include it as a real benefit. Meals and entertainment are similar to travel in that they must be reasonable and necessary to business. You can only deduct 50% of the cost if you can show they have a beneficial effect and can you can reasonably show you expect more income or business from the customer.

Summary of Biggest IRS Approved Benefits

Medical Reimbursement Plan	$ 10,000+
Retirement	$ 52,000
Hire Your Child (per child)	$ 6,100
Insurance	$ 500-4,000
Education	$ 5,250
Dependent care Assistance	$ 5,000
Vehicle	$ 3,000-6000
Total	$ 80,000+

What a possible bonanza just for structuring and documenting your corporate activities properly. Of course, you may not be able to use all the dollar benefits, but certainly a major portion of them would be available to you.

.

Needless to say, your business must produce the revenue to be able to take advantage of the benefits, but that would be the case with any form of business. If you don't utilize the above benefits and still produce the amount of net income, you will be paying tax on the above forgone benefits.

For more complete details of the above and twenty other possible specific corporate tax "loopholes" for closely owned corporations, see my book "CASH OUT" @ Amazon.com.

Chapter 6

Raising Money for Your Business

In this chapter we will give you a brief overview of ways to raise money for your iCorporation. It is meant to give you direction and point you to those who are experienced in this field.

Warning. You must be careful soliciting money for your business. The more people you involve as investors, the more complicated and risky it becomes. Securities law is extremely complicated. You need an experienced professional to guide you through the maze of selling stock, especially when it comes to soliciting money from people you do not know.

An iCorporation is the ideal entity to raise money from more than just a handful of investors. The ownership interests are easily divisible and can be clearly defined. When you sell ownership interest in your iCorporation you sell shares of stock. For the purposes of this discussion the words "shares" and "stock" are synonymous. If your company has 100,000 shares and you sell 10,000 to an investor they would own 10% of your company.

Whether you are an existing Corporation with years of operations, which needs money for a major expansion, or just have an idea and want to bring together investors to develop that idea, the corporate form will work just fine. Remember, you will lose all privacy when you offer stock to investors. Almost everything about your company will have to be disclosed.

Almost all public solicitation of money is regulated by the United States Securities and Exchange Commission (SEC) or state laws. Most of these laws were created in the 1930's to prevent the public from being scammed out of their money. This is extremely serious business. If you do not follow the rules and regulations you can wind up in **jail**.

Founder's stock.

Founder's stock is the initial shares that are issued to the founders of the iCorporation in exchange for their initial investment in the Corporation. Let's say that your Articles of Incorporation initially called for 1 million shares to be issued at $.01 cent per share. That would equal $10,000 in initial capital. This is the $10,000 that you use to get things started. The amount of money that you initially put into the company would depend entirely on what your projected needs are in your business plan. A simple service company might only need a few thousand dollars to set up its offices, purchase stationery and supplies. A new automobile company may require tens of millions of dollars in initial capital.

Capitalization is the term for funding your venture. Let's see how capitalization affects your ownership.

You have a simple lawn maintenance company and $10,000 would be enough to get you started. You would own all 1 million shares at $.01 per share, or 100% of the company. Let's say a friend decides he wants to be a part owner and he approaches you to invest in your new venture. You and your friend negotiate for him to invest $5,000 and you agree to give him 10% or 100,000 shares. The situation now stands that you own 90% of the company and your friend owns 10% of the company, and the company still has $10,000 in the bank. Because you sold 100,000 shares of your one million, that $5,000 your friend invested goes to you.

An alternative method of capitalizing the company would result in a different ownership percentage for each of you. It would go as follows: the company's total has 1 million shares. Both you and your friend each to put in $5,000 each and split the share ownership 500,000 shares each. Now each of you own 50% of the company and the company has $10,000 in the bank.

Let me illustrate yet a third alternative. Let's say you need $10,000 to get started. Again the Articles of Incorporation call for 1 million shares at one cent each. But this time, you purchased 500,000 of the 1 million shares for one cent each for $5,000 and you agree with the Corporation that you will loan it $5000, to be paid back under the terms of a note with the iCorporation. Now the company has $10,000 to work with, part equity and part loan. You now only own one half (500,000 shares) of the total authorized shares. Since there are no other stockholders you still own 100% of the company, and the company still has the other 500,000 shares to sell to a possible investor. As you sell shares you ownership percentage is diluted.

The company can't borrow all the money. You must put in enough equity capital to legitimately fund your operations to avoid a piercing the corporate veil claim.

As you can see, how you capitalize the company has a dramatic effect on its ownership.

Regardless of how you do the initial capitalization of the Corporation, these are founder's shares. At this point only you and your friend are risking your money. If you are going to sell your shares or any of the company's remaining shares to other people, it becomes the subject of outside regulation to some degree.

Private placements-friends and family

Let's say you started your lawn business with $5,000 in initial capital and a $5,000 loan to the iCorporation. You're doing well, but you need to purchase additional equipment to expand your services. Your brother-in-law and neighbor see that you are doing well and are making some money. They express an interest. You show them the company finances and describe your business operations. Since you need to buy additional equipment and they have some money to invest, you offer to sell each person 50,000 company shares for $2,000 each. Now the company has $4,000 more as working capital, but you now have three stockholders and reduced ownership

New ownership is 50,0000 shares divided by 1,000,000 = 5% ownership each for a total of 10%. You now have 90% ownership.

This is the most rudimentary form of a private placement. You disclose your business operations and finances to the possible investor; the investor assesses the risk of investing with you; and you negotiate the amount of money and the number of shares that you will exchange.

Even at this stage there may be some state regulatory requirements. At this point you are now playing with other people's money and you need the advice of an attorney that knows security law.

Private placements can be tiny, like the one illustrated above, or can be for millions of dollars. They must follow the limited guidelines of no public solicitation or advertising, limited to less than 35 investors and provide disclosure of the company activities through a business plan. It would describe operations, legal organization, finances, risks and future plans.

You will need a written stock subscription agreement that says that the investors have investigated the investment opportunity, have reviewed the materials, were aware of the risks and have made their own decision to invest. The subscription agreement will also detail the number of shares and the amount of money invested.

The most important aspect of a subscription agreement is that it acts as proof, to help protect you from the investors. It says they have been informed of the operations, finances, future plans, and most importantly the risks of the investment. It is important to remember that they approached you.

It is not the purview of this book to get into the ramifications of *public* offering of stock. Here are some of the exemptions from public registration under the Securities Act of 1933 and the Securities Exchange Act 1934 for further research. They will allow you to raise money without a full blown public registration offer:

1. Small Offerings

2. Intrastate Offerings

3. Private Placements

4. Regulation D Offerings

There is an important concept of "accredited investors" that appears throughout the regulations. You usually can only sell to accredited investors which are defined as:

85

- a bank, insurance company, registered investment company, business development company, or small business investment Company;
- an employee benefit plan, within the meaning of the employee retirement income securities act;
- a charitable organization, corporation or partnership with assets of more than $5 million;
- a director, executive officer, or general partner of the company selling the securities;
- a business in which all the equity owners are accredited investors, a natural person with a net worth of at least $1 million;
- a natural person with income exceeding $200,000 in each of the two most recent years or joint income with the spouse exceeding $300,000, with a reasonable expectation of the same income level in the current year;
- a trust with assets of at least $5 million, not formed to acquire the securities offered, or those purchased are directed by a sophisticated person.

As you can see, the securities law requires that you only sell to people who have substantial means and investment sophistication.

Small Offerings-Regulation A

The Securities Act authorizes the exemption, under Regulation A, for registration of small securities offering. This exemption allows public offerings not to exceed $5 million in any 12 month period. If you want to rely on this exemption, your company must file an offering statement with the SEC for review.

Regulation A offerings are similar to registered public offerings but have significantly easier specifications. You must provide purchasers with an offering circular that is similar in content to a prospectus. The securities can be offered publicly and are not "restricted" meaning they are freely traded and available in the secondary market after the offering. The principal advantages of a Regulation A offering are:

- The financial statements are similar, but don't have to be audited.
- There are no Exchange Act reporting obligations after the offering unless the company has more than $10 million in total assets and 500 or more shareholders.
- The company may prepare an offering circular in a simplified question-and-answer document.

- Finally you may "test the waters" to determine if there is a enough interest in your securities before going to the expense of filing with the SEC. To test the waters you may use general solicitation and advertising to judge the interest of your securities, but you cannot accept money until the SEC staff completes its review of your filed offering statement and your delivery of prescribed material to investors.

Intrastate offering exemption

There is one other exemption under the Securities Act, section 3(3)(11). To qualify for the intrastate offering exemption your company must:

- be incorporated in the state where it is offering the securities;
- carry out a significant amount of its business in that state;
- make offers and sales only to residents of that state.

There is no fixed limit on the size of the offering or the number of purchasers. Your company must determine the residence of each purchaser. If any of the securities are offered or sold to even one out of state person, the exemption pay be lost. Without exemption, the company would be in violation of the Securities Act.

If the purchaser resells any of the securities to persons who reside outside the state, the entire transaction might violate securities laws.

It is difficult for your company to rely on the intrastate state exemption unless you know the purchasers and negotiate directly with them. If your company holds some of its assets outside the state, or derives a substantial portion of its revenue outside the state, it will probably have a difficult time qualifying for this exemption.

Private Placements

There are two types of private placements, Regulation D and Small Corporation Offering Registration (SCOR).

Private placement of securities is exempt from federal registration. In 1982, the SEC adopted Regulation D, Rule 506, which set forth the rules for exemptions from federal registration. Under rules 504, 505 and 506 of

Regulation D they spell out cost and time saving methods for small business to raise capital from private investors.

Regulation D Offerings

There are three separate exemptions from the Securities Act registration:

Rule 504 provides an exemption for the offer and sale of up to $1 million of securities in a 12 month period. Like other Regulation D exemptions, in general you may not use public solicitation or advertising to market the securities. The investors receive "restricted" securities, meaning they may not sell the securities to others without registration. However, you may use this exemption for public offerings and then investors will receive freely traded securities under the following conditions:

- You register the offering exclusively in one or more states that require a publicly filed registration statement and delivery of a disclosure document to investors;
- You register and sell in the state that requires registration and disclosure delivery and sale in the state without those requirements, so long as you deliver the disclosure documents required by the state in which you registered to all purchasers;

- You sell exclusively according to state law exemptions that permit general solicitation and advertising, so long as you sell only to accredited investors, as defined above.

Even if you make a private sale where there is no specific disclosure required, you should take care to provide sufficient information to investors to avoid violating the anti-fraud provisions of securities laws. This means that any information you provide to investors must be free from false and misleading statements. Also, you should not exclude any information if the omission makes it false or misleading.

SCOR-Small Company Offering Registration

SCOR was created to facilitate the raising of capital by coordinating states so they can follow similar rules. SCOR offerings operate under the SEC Rule 504. The federal and state governments each have their own securities laws. Your company must comply with both state and federal laws. Just because an offering is exempt under federal law does not necessarily mean it's exempt under state law.

Each state requires registration and review of your offering.

SCOR offerings are done by each state with over 45 states recognizing them. SCOR offerings are done through a simplified question-and-answer registration form that discloses information to investors. The advantage of this type of offering is that it can be advertised, have no accredited investor requirements, and can even be listed for trading. The amount of money is limited to $1 million in any one 12 month period.

Rule 505 provides an exemption for offers of securities totaling up to $5 million in any one 12 month period. Under this exemption, you may sell stock to a limited number of "accredited investors" and up to 35 other persons who need not satisfy the sophistication and wealth standards associated with the other exemptions. Purchasers must buy for investment only, not for resale. The securities that are issued are "restricted", meaning you must inform investors that the stocks may not be sold for at least one year without registering the transaction. You also may not use general solicitation or advertising to sell the securities.

Financial statements under this rule need to be certified by an independent public accountant. If the company cannot obtain audited financial statements without unreasonable effort and expense only the company's balance sheet must be audited and current 120 days from the start of the offering. Limited partnerships unable to obtain required financial statements without unreasonable effort or expense may furnish unaudited financial statements prepared under federal income tax laws.

Rule 506 is a" safe harbor" for private offering exemption. If your company satisfies the following standards you can be assured that you are within the Section 4(2) exemption:

- you can raise an unlimited amount of capital;

- you cannot use general solicitation or advertising to market the securities;
- you can sell securities to an unlimited number of accredited investors and up to 35 other purchasers. They must have sufficient knowledge and experience in business and financial matters to enable them to evaluate the merits and risk;

- It is up to you to decide what information you give to accredited investors, so long as it does not violate the anti-fraud prohibitions, but you must give non-accredited investors disclosure documents that are the same as registered offerings;
- You must be available to answer questions by prospective purchasers; financial statements are requires under the same as in rule 505;
- Purchasers receive "restricted" securities that may not be freely trade after the offering.

Although this is a quick overview of ways to raise money from outside investors, it's obvious that this is a very complicated area of the law, and that you need professional, experienced help.

Do not attempt to raise money from the public without sound professional advice.

Loans

 To this point we have been talking about raising money by selling stock to investors, which as previously discussed, has many and sometimes severe legal requirements. Borrowing from the public has the same legal restrictions as equity offerings.

You can also borrow money, either from private parties or from banks. Creating a loan has both advantages and disadvantages for small companies. You must judge whether borrowing is better for your situation than selling stock.

Bank borrowing is tough. Only 11.7% of small business loans were approved by large banks, and only 47.5% were approved by small banks in 2011.

Let's look at the advantages of debt versus equity.

1. The lender does not have a claim on your business equity. In other words the lender doesn't own any of your stock, and therefore does not dilute the ownership interest in your business. The lender

only gets the interest and the principle repaid, with no claim on the share of your profits. When paid it is simple to end the relationship.

2. You usually do not have a lender who wants to make "suggestions" on how to operate your business. You are not obligated to hold regular meetings, get votes of shareholders or provide regular reports. Whereas stockholders usually do have some kind of say in running the business even if it's a minority interest.

3. In most cases, borrowing money does not require entanglements with state and federal securities laws. But remember if you're offering debt securities to the public you must be in compliance with state and federal regulations.

4. Since you know the terms of the loan you can budget both the principal and interest payments so it is clear how much it will cost you.

There are, of course, some disadvantages of debt over equity.

1. In negotiating the loan, you may have to pledge some of your company's assets to serve as collateral. You may have to personally guarantee the loan. The lender may even want you to pledge

some of your personal assets. This is a very dangerous thing to do. If you personally guaranteed loans, you lose one of the greatest advantages of your corporate form. You now become personally responsible for repaying the loan if the company cannot.

2. Banks and many other private lenders will not loan you money unless you have clear and sufficient collateral to ensure that the loans will be repaid. Even if you have sufficient collateral, many times the bank will not entertain a loan because if your venture fails, or you fail to repay the loan, they do not want to go through the legal entanglements to collect on your collateral.

3. Of course, you must qualify to the standards that the lenders set. Be sure you have adequate credit scores before you even attempt a bank loan. Loans must be repaid and interest on a loan becomes an additional expense that your company's operations must cover. The repayment often drains company cash flow. The interest you're paying could be used to make additional investments in the business.

4. Some lenders may impose some restrictions on your operations. They don't want you borrowing additional money if it, in any way, threatens their principal and interest repayment.

Whether you borrow money or sell stocks, it is critically important for you to have clear, accurate financial statements and other documentation for full disclosure of your business activities. Good financial statements and other documentation created a strong impression of your knowledge and control of the business.

Small Business Administration (SBA)

There is a lot of hype about getting loans from the SBA. The federal government overstates the ease and leniency requirements to get these loans. SBA loans are merely bank loans which have a federal guarantee if the bank follows the guidelines set forth by the SBA. You must go through the same qualification requirements as a regular business loan, but since there is federal backing, it is usually a little bit easier to obtain.

There are three separate loan programs available at the SBA.

7(a) Loan Program is the primary program to help small business. The loan proceeds can be used for normal business purposes such as working capital, equipment, fixtures, furniture, land, renovations, improvements and building purchase.

Loan terms extend up to 25 years. These loans are aimed at start-ups and existing small business and are granted through commercial lenders. Talk to your bank about using 7(a) loans to fund your business.

Certified Development Company Loans (CDC504) program is primarily focused on fixed assets, real estate and improvements. The funds are provided by Certified Development Companies. The loans are secured by senior liens for up to 25 years on the fixed assets. They require at least a 10% contribution from the borrower.

Microloan Program loans are intended for small business and Not for Profit childcare centers. The loans are provided through nonprofit lending organizations that also provide technical assistance and management advice. These loans are for less than $50,000 and used for working capital, furniture, fixtures, equipment. The proceeds can not be used to pay existing debt or real estate.

If you want the government in your business, this is the way to go.

For all programs, you will need a good business plan and complete formal financial statements. You go through a lengthy application process to assess your character, credit, business experience and reliability.

Contact the SBA at www.sba.gov

Crowd Funding

Crowd funding is a new, innovative method to raise money. Essentially you offer your ideas over the world-wide Internet to potentially millions of people who may have an interest in what you're doing. This kind of funding is used to gather money for diverse activities, such as movie production, software development, artists' projects, disaster relief, political issues, company startups, creation of toys, books and inventions.

Generally, you are asking for financial support from strangers who would like to support your idea usually in exchange for the product or just altruisic purposes. Although in most cases the promoter asks for small amounts, from $5.00 to $50.00, in some instances the promoter may be asking for contributions of several thousand dollars. There is no guarantee the project will be successful or any promise to repay the contributions.

The best way to fully understand crowd funding is to go to Kickstart.com, CrowdFunding.com, Growthink.com or Indiegogo.com for examples of the kind and scope of crowd funding.

For our purposes let's look at recent developments in crowd funding for equity.

EquityCrowdFunding.com is a bit different from most crowd funding activities in that you are offering equity in a company. Because you are selling stock, the government gets involved to "protect" the investor. As part of the JOBS Act of 2012, companies can use Crowd Funding to sell small amounts of stock equity to many investors with fewer restrictions than traditional equity funding.

Investors can then purchase a small piece of the company. The value of the stock may raise or fall depending on the success or failure of the venture. There is generally no public, liquid market for these shares.

Most people can participate if they don't commit more than $2,000 and 5% of their annual income or net worth, if either their net worth or annual income is less than $100,000.

Companies seeking to raise less than $100,000 need only have to have the principal officer certify their financial statement is correct.

Companies seeking $100,000 to $500,000 are required to have a public account review the financial statement. Those wanting over $500,000 need to have an audited financial statement.

All companies must provide operational results no less than annually and be subject to liblity for "material mis-statement".

It will probably take a minimum of $10,000 to raise "Crowd" funds.

As usually, the minute the government gets involved in "protecting "us, the costs and paperwork will skyrocket.

The JOBS Act legislation requires that funding portals and broker dealers be registered with the Securities Exchange Commission. The legislation restricts amounts and qualification of investors who are allowed to invest in any 12 month period. Currently, issuers may offer up to $1 million of stock in a 12 month period. The Financial Industry Authority is also creating rules for its member firms to follow.

Several organizations have been created to provide education and information in equity funding. They include: Crowdfunding Professional Association, National Crowdfunding Assocation, and Crowdfunding Intermediary Regulatory Advocates.

To get around the equity restrictions, you might ask the "Crowd" to directly fund a project that your company is developing. For example, let's say you are developing a new software program. In exchange for their contribution you might offer a copy of the program to each contributor when finished. This way you are not diluting your equity and you get the money that the equity funding was going to fund anyway.

Credit

While we are on the subject of getting money for your business, it is fundamental that you establish a good *business* credit file. Go to Dun and Bradstreet (D&B) (www.sba.gov)to establish an account in your iCorporation's name. Remember you are separate from the iCorporation. Do not be nervous if you have had personal credit problems in the past. The account is all about your business credit, not you personally.

You will get a DUNS number for your business. A DUNS number is a Data Universal Numbering System that is a unique number identifier that has become the industry standard for business listings worldwide. You register your business and you will begin to build a business credit profile that is based on the 4 C's. They are:

Character includes such things as size, location, number of years in business, business structure, number of employees, history of principals, liens, judgments and comments from references.

Capacity assesses the ability of a business to pay its bills, its cash flow, the company's debt, and the existence of unused credit.

Capital assesses whether a company has the financial resources to repay their creditors. Heavy weighting is given to such balance sheet items as working capital, net worth and cash flow.

Conditions consider the external factors surrounding a business under consideration, such as influences as market fluctuations, industry growth and political factors.

This sounds very daunting for new businesses. But you start small and build. This is very important to vendors, banks, and other lenders. Many times vendors check your D&B rating without your knowledge. You begin by opening small accounts with vendors and establish a good payment record. It is not unusual to be able to get $30,000 to $100,000 credit within six months.

Jeremy Zigman has an excellent program to guide you through establishing corporate credit. mailto:http://bitly.com/BusinessCreditWebinar/dean

Chapter 7

Strategies

 This chapter will describe a few examples of ways to structure your business for maximum tax savings and at the same time protect your investment and assets. They will lower your liability and limit your potential losses. Even the smallest business can use some of these strategies.

To justify the use of these strategies you should always keep in mind that your sole purpose should not be just tax avoidance. There should be legitimate and solid business reasons to implement them. Additional reasons might be to limit liability, increase profit or margins, or reduce lawsuit probability, etc. You must document those reasons and include them in your corporate minutes. And finally, be sure to take all actions and measures to put them in place. For example, get the required licenses, permits, contracts or documents.

There are dozens of strategies, depending on your business circumstances. Let's examine just five to get a broad outline of the possibilities.

Strategy #1

Rent your house, condo or vacation home to your iCorporation for periodic meetings. IRS code section 280A(g) allows you to rent your property for less than 15 days per year and received the income tax free. As long as it is a legitimate business expense, your iCorporation can deduct it.

Assume you rent a hotel room for a periodic business meeting, either for planning or corporate meetings. This is quite common and is actually required by corporate by-laws to have a minimum of at least one meeting per year. Let's say you meet monthly. The room would cost you $500 per day at the nearby Hilton. Twelve times $500 per day will cost the iCorporation $6,000 a year, a business deduction. You do this at the hotel to avoid normal business interruptions during the day, or for other reasons. You must put the reasons for the meeting in your corporate minutes. Also get proof of the reasonableness of the rental rate from the hotel. You take these steps to substantiate your business reasons and the charges.

Using the above example, you rent your house to the iCorporation instead of the hotel room. Obviously, this is quite aggressive, but clearly within the regulations of the IRS code. You must take all the steps above to substantiate the transaction between two separate entities, you and the iCorporation.

Results for owners of a regular iCorporation: You get up to 14 days of rental income tax free, in this case $6,000, and the iCorporation gets a reduction from its taxable income and therefore a reduction in corporate tax of 15% or more, depending on its final tax bracket.

Results for an S corporation: You get up to 14 days rental income tax free and the corporation, which passes both income and expense through to your personal tax return, thereby reducing your personal tax liability.

Outside the corporate venue, you might use this 14 day loophole to capture rental income for your well located home or vacation properties.

This one strategy is used annually by homeowners around Augusta National Golf course and other golf venues to produce thousands of dollars of tax free income in a short two week period. Homeowners in Olympic venue cities have also successfully used this profit strategy.

I learned this one from Jeff Schneppers insightful book, How to Pay Zero Taxes.

Strategy #2

Create a iCorporation in corporate tax free Nevada and have the iCorporation own rights to books, software, software applications, music, copy writes, or patents. The fees for these rights and uses are paid to a tax friendly state.

Results: It would save on your home state corporate taxes, which could range from 2-10%. With proper contacts between the iCorporation and the product creator, the earnings could be paid out from iCorporations as royalties or dividends. Royalties and dividends are not subject to self employment taxes. Dividends, as of this writing, are subject to lower tax rates than most regular earned income.

Apple Computers, Microsoft Corporation, Cisco and others have subsidiary corporations in Nevada to take advantage of this arrangement. Apple and others create this arrangement in Luxembourg to avoid many European taxes.

Google has been reported to have over $8 billion in Caribbean based subsidiaries corporations, saving over $2 billion in taxes. In December 2012, when questioned about this arrangement, Eric Schmidt, the CEO, said "the government has set up incentives for companies to operate there (in foreign countries)". He is right. You should utilize as many taxes breaks that are written to the law as you can.

Strategy #3

Buy or hold domestic dividend paying stocks in your iCorporation.

Part of the dividends are excluded from the gross income of the iCorporation. An iCorporation is eligible to deduct dividends it receives in three different categories.

If your Corporation owns more than 80% of the corporation paying the dividend, it is taxed at a zero rate, i.e. 100% excluded from income. If your iCorporation owns at least 20% , but less than 80% of the stock paying the dividend, 80% of the dividend is excluded from the corporation receiving the dividend. If your iCorporation owns less than 20% of the company paying the dividend, then 70% of the paid dividend is excluded from gross income of the receiving corporation.

If you are above the zero to 15% personal tax bracket, this becomes a hugely beneficial way to own stocks. If the federal government raises the dividend rate for the 10-15% bracket it becomes an even a larger advantage.

Just be careful not to be classified as a "personal holding" company. That classification is achieved when more than 60% of the corporation's income is passive income such as dividends, interest, royalties, rents and annuities and personal service contracts, and five or few individuals own 50 percent of the outstanding stock.

You can fail the test (and you want to), by simply selling enough products to change the percentage ratios or move enough rental income into the iCorporation to change the income ratio to less than 60%.

If you qualify as a personal holding company then you lose the above tax advantages and pay taxes at the regular corporate rates PLUS 20%.

Talk with an accountant that understands the personal holding company rules.

Strategy #4

This is a story of two corporations that do business together, just like millions of others.

One is in California, a high tax state (or any other high tax state). The other one is in Nevada, a no income tax state.

The California company incorporates and goes into the retail furniture business, or it could be in almost any business. They incorporate in their home state of California (or any home state) with a calendar year S corporation.

The owners go to the bank to borrow money to buy inventory, fixtures and equipment to establish the business. But the bank wants a personal guarantee and some of the owner's property to guarantee repayment. The California owner does not want to risk all of his personal assets, and lose the protection of the corporate form, so he looks for another source of financing.

The California owner finds a Nevada company that is willing to loan the money he needs. All the Nevada company wants is an on demand promissory note at 15% interest, a security lien as collateral on the assets the California company, and a Universal Commercial Code filing (UCC −1) to let the world know the California company is indebted to the Nevada company. The UCC statement is filed as a public document in California to let everyone know that the Nevada company has the first lien on all the assets pledged. The loan must be paid before anyone else can get the assets of the California company.

The California corporation borrows $100,000 and agrees to pay $15,000 or 15%, interest on the money borrowed (these numbers are for example only and can be for any amounts). The interest becomes an expense to the California company and is paid to the Nevada company. Since the California furniture company only makes $15,000 in net profit before interest in the first year, it has to pay out $15,000 of it in interest, and it has no profit for the year. It might even lose money, which is not necessarily a disaster, because it is an S Corporation. Those loses can be written off against other personal income. The company pays no income taxes, just the minimal fees California charges each year for a Corporation.

If the Nevada company agrees, the California company could even finance its retail customers with on-time payment plans. The California company would sell the contracts to the Nevada company and the Nevada company earns interest on those contracts.

It doesn't appear that this is a very good business. It goes to a lot of trouble, risk and effort to make no money. But let's assume one more thing.

You and your family own BOTH corporations.

Now let's look at the results of this ownership. The California corporation makes no money and pays virtually no income taxes. The California corporation is almost worthless, because the money it makes goes to the Nevada iCorporation, thereby making it a poor lawsuit target. Its assets are pledged as collateral. It is for all practical purposes, a lawsuit proof company.

After all, if the Corporation is sued, the attorneys for the plaintiff will investigate and find out that there is virtually nothing to go after. It would cost the plaintiff a lot of money in attorney's fees and costs. Probably, the attorney would not take it on a contingency basis. If the attorney proceeds anyway, and wins a judgment, all they would be getting is a company that owes a lot of money. So why bother.

The Nevada Corporation is very low risk because it is the California company owned by you or your family. You are not likely to sue yourself.

The Nevada Corporation makes $15,000 in interest, less a few minor expenses. The income is earned in a no corporate income tax state. All it pays is a few nominal annual fees.

The Nevada company could also be earning interest from the California company's retail customer financing contracts. Also, it could be earning interest from other companies' retail financings. This is great for used auto dealerships, furniture retailers, dental and vision practices, real estate notes and any where financing is needed.

You could set up a similar arrangement between the California (or any home state company) and the Nevada iCorporation to purchase any products or services. For example, you could buy advertising through your Nevada iCorporation advertising agency, or marketing or consulting services, finance equipment leasing, or new product development.

Your business reasons for setting up such an arrangement are to spread risk, provide enhanced liability protection, enhance privacy, and as a side benefit, reduce your taxes.

Federal tax returns would be filed as a usual. State taxes would be filed and no income taxes would be due in Nevada because there is no corporate income tax. No income taxes would be due in California, because there is no profit.

Of course, you want to be sure that all the appropriate notes, documents and agreements are signed and filed in the appropriate manner. The documentation is the proof that the business is carried on between two independent legal entities.

Strategy #5

If your iCorporation is a S Corporation (see #7 FAQ), one that passed through all the profit/loss to your personal tax return, you could reduce or eliminate the social security (FICA) and Medicare (MC) taxes.

Currently the FICA tax is 12.4%,(6.2% paid by the corporation, 6.2% paid by the employee by to $113,700). The

MC tax is 2.9%, the employer and employee each pay 1.45% each.

The total FICA and MC is 15.3%.

So, on a $100,000 salary, the tax would be $15,300 in payroll taxes.

If you were not paid any salary there would be NO payroll taxes, a $15,300 savings. You could still provide a yearly living expense by taking the $100,000 out of the corporate earnings as a profit dividend that is passed on via the K-1 form to your personal tax return. These earnings would be considered dividends, which by law, have no FICA or MC tax on them. The $100,000 would still be taxed as income.

So, you say, that is a great way to save $15,300, BUT the IRS is not stupid-they see this strategy as the tax dodge it is. Therefore, they don't allow you to do it.

However, you can be reasonable and still partly utilize the strategy. You must pay yourself, as an employee, a "reasonable wage". A "reasonable wage" is not a straight forward calculation and is subject to a wide range of "reasonableness". The amount you are paid depends on a number of factors including:

- Training and experience
- Duties and responsibilities
- Time and effort devoted to the business
- Dividend history
- Other payment to non-shareholder employees
- Timing and manner of paying bonuses to key people
- What comparable businesses pay
- Compensation agreement
- What is the formula to determine compensation

The IRS will also look at amounts paid to family members to determine reasonableness.

Example 1: the company earns $200,000 (after all expense and salary). You, the owner are only paid $10,000 in salary (to avoid payroll taxes) and another $90,000 in dividends. The IRS would not accept this split because it is not reasonable and an obvious attempt to avoid payroll taxes.

Example 2: Same circumstances as above, but this time you are paid $95,000 and include the other reasonableness factors. This would probably be acceptable, but has the advantage of still saving a over $5,000 in payroll taxes. This example is similar to a court case in February 2012 that was held as "reasonable".

These are just a few examples of strategies that could be put to use. The iCorporation could be used in combination with limited partnerships, limited liability companies (LLCs), offshore corporations, and trusts for even greater privacy and protection.

The author is not offering tax or legal advice, only reciting numerous examples of strategies that have been used over the years. Do not believe anyone that tells you they can eliminate all your tax obligations. The IRS says, that as a US citizen, you are responsible for income earned worldwide within the bounds of US tax law. Tax law is ridiculously complex and subject to interpretation. It is up to you and your accountant to report correctly.

Chapter 8

Where Should I Incorporate?

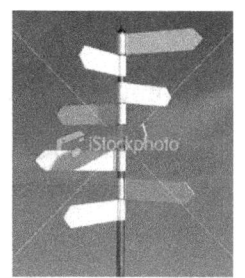 The best place to incorporate is where you get the greatest advantages after considering all the factors in your particular kind of business.

You want to take in to consideration all the factors that would affect your business.

What kind of business are you in? Are you in small retail, manufacturing, international business, services, mail-order or Internet? Where is most of your business coming from or anticipated to come from? What are the taxes and regulations? What are the environmental restrictions? What kind of labor pool do you need? Is there a pro-business atmosphere? Do you provide financing? Are shipping costs important? Is your business in a high risk category, like contracting, restaurants or manufacturing? What is your net worth? What strategies are there to reduce risk, protect your personal assets, or save taxes?

For example, if you have a small retail store selling clothing, most of your business is going to come from local customers, with local suppliers; you have no need for customer financing or services. Your choice would probably be to incorporate in your home state.

On the other hand, if your business is primarily conducted on the Internet you could be incorporated almost anywhere. Reliable communications and shipping may be more important to you.

An important consideration for where to incorporate is where is the nexus of your business? Nexus means the connections your business has to a state. The nexus determines if you are "doing business" in that state. The term "doing business" is imprecise. Each state is a bit different, and some are more aggressive than others to connect your company to the state. They want more of your income. Nexus factors can include where the sales take place; where was the order taken and approved; where was the order fulfilled; do you have offices in the state, or employees; is there service for the product in the state; do you maintaining facilities, such as a warehouse? All these factors and more determine the nexus.

Interstate commerce is regulated by the Federal government. So, just because you sell something in the state from another state does not mean you have corporate nexus in that state. Financing and soliciting orders through independent contractors are exempt for the nexus theory. There are many other activities that are not considered "doing business". Public Law 86-272 ,which has been adopted by all the states, generally outlines if you have enough nexus to be considered as "doing business" in a state. If you "do business" in that state, it requires you to register and become subject to its income tax and corporate regulations.

Even if you incorporate in Nevada and then qualify in your home state as a "foreign corporation", you still have the benefits of extremely friendly courts and laws of Nevada. But when you register in the home state you lose your privacy and many of the tax advantages.

Nevada

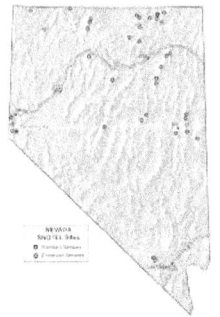

The author has a preference for Nevada incorporations because of the many advantages built into Nevada law.

The Nevada story is unique because it was built primarily to attract businesses with its corporate laws. Until 1859 Nevada was just a United States territory people traveled through to get to California. When vast quantities of silver were discovered adventurous, independent opportunity seekers flooded in. In 1864 Nevada became a state. It became a synonymous with the "Wild West". Nevada laws reflected this independence in the creation of legalized gambling, prostitution and quickie divorces. Gambling was developed during the 1960s and 1970s into a huge industry that brought tourism and many more permanent residents.

Nevada realized it could not just depend on gambling and tourism. It began to look for other ways to attract business. In the 1980's Nevada started to put into place corporate laws to attract more business. One of those industries that developed from that business friendly attitude has become the corporate support business. Today, there are more than 126,00 active corporations that call Nevada home. In 2012, there were over 17,000 new corporate filings with the Secretary of State. Let's look at some of the Nevada laws that make Nevada such a great place to incorporate a business.

Many states have some of the positive elements of Nevada, but only Nevada brings them *all* together to create a superior business friendly environment. Even the Nevada Secretary of State's office publishes materials touting these many advantages.

- Nevada has no state personal income tax. The ban on income tax is actually in the Constitution making it very difficult to change. Only six other states have no personal state income tax.
- There is no corporate income tax. Other states have corporate income taxes that range from 1% to 10%.
- There is no franchise tax and just as importantly no voluminous annual reports of disclosure on many aspects of the business.
- Nevada is the only state that does not have an information sharing agreement with the IRS.

Because there is no state or corporate income tax the state does not share information with the federal government. Many other states routinely share records with the IRS to verify state tax returns.

- The Secretary of State's office has very low annual fees. At this writing, there is a $200 state business license tax and $125 annual fee for listing officers and directors. The initial fee to set up your Articles of Incorporation is only $75.

- There is very little reporting required by the state. Once a year the state requires a single page report with the names and addresses of corporate officers, directors and a local resident agent. A person can be a nominee, thereby making the officers, directors, and stockholders anonymous. Our office provides nominee services for a small annual fee.

- There is no minimum capital required.

- Stockholders are not listed as part of the public record.

- Stockholders, directors and officers need not live in Nevada or even be US citizens.

- Official corporate meetings can be held anywhere, or by phone.

- One person corporations can be set up. All officers and directors may be filled by a single person.

- Nevada corporations may issue stock for capital, services, personal property, real estate and the directors may determine the value of these transactions.

- A corporation can be set up very quickly. Our company sets up corporations in usually 7-10 days, but it can be done in as little as 2 hours, with the payment of state expedited fees.

- Nevada corporations can own property in any state.

- Nevada law shields officers and stockholders from personal liability. Outright fraud is the only reason Nevada allows outsiders to pierce the corporate veil.

- The Articles of Incorporation can eliminate any personal liability for officers and directors, except in the case of improper payment of dividends.

- When incorporated in Nevada, Nevada law governs the rules in lawsuits.

- Nevada law allows for the issuance of bearer shares. In other words, whoever holds the share certificates owns the shares. The only information required on certificates is the name of the Corporation, the number of shares, a signature of an officer or agent certifying the shares.

- There is no requirement that a Nevada Corporation conduct active business. It can be set up simply to hold property, patents, royalty rights, other passive assets and income derived from them.

Each of these above points has its own ramifications and uses. Our firm helps you structure the iCorporation to take advantage of Nevada's unique laws.

Chapter 9

Questions Most People Ask.

1. What is the cost to incorporate?

   The cost varies with each state. The state fees to file Articles of Incorporation are as little as $50 in Wyoming to several hundred in others. Call your state's Secretary of State and ask. The cost to complete all the documentation after the state filing will depend on who does the work for you. Attorneys have their own individual rates. Many online "do it yourself" services charge in the neighborhood of $400-$500. Much of the cost depends on any extra services, customization of Bylaws, the quality of corporate books, and stock certificates. Subsequent annual state fees can range from $100 to as much as$800 in California.

2. How long does it take to set up a corporation?

   Some states, like, Nevada and California, offer expatiated services that can be as little as several hours. The usual time is one to two weeks.

The filing of the Article of Incorporation is the simplest step. Before you file be sure to do some planning. Our office provides a 26 point questionnaire to help you with that planning.

3. What is the difference between officers, directors and stockholders? Stockholders are the owners of the corporation. They select the directors to set policy and make the decisions about the direction of the company. The directors also hire the officers. The officers carry out the day to day actions to run the company. The duties of the officers are described by the corporate Bylaws. The usual officers are the President, which oversees the overall operations. The Secretary takes care of the corporate books, records the minutes of the meetings, takes care of all the formalities to keep the company in good standing with the state. The Treasurer usually is responsible for the company financial books. In Nevada, one person can hold all the offices.

The directors may appoint additional officers, like vice presidents if they choose.

4. What is a registered agent? All states require a resident agent to be physically present within the state. The agent must have an actual street address, no PO boxes. The agent must be a natural person over 18 years of age. Each state has its own requirements for the duties of the resident agent as to the documents they must keep. The purpose of a registered agent is to provide a place where any legal papers or notices can be served. Our office provides a service for Nevada corporations for a small annual fee.

5. What are Bylaws? Bylaws are a set of guidelines and rules to govern the Corporation. They are created and agreed on by the stockholders and directors at the initial meeting after the Corporation is formed. It is the operations manual for the Corporation. Bylaws should spell out :
   a. Time and date of annual meeting.
   b. Define a voting quorum for shareholders.
   c. A procedure for changing the bylaws.

d. How to elect and replace directors and officers.

e. And any other items that the directors and stockholders agree on that still fall within state regulations.

6. What are resolutions? Resolutions authorize and direct the officers, directors and the company to take all sorts of actions. They are agreed on in writing by the directors and should be permanently placed in the corporate books. Here is a list of significant decisions that definitely should have approved resolutions :
-Changing directors and officers.

-Opening bank accounts.

-Issuing stock.

-Taking or giving a corporate loan.

-Authorizing fringe benefits.

-Set up retirement plans

-Capitalizing the corporation

-Contracts with third parties

-Contracts with inside parties

7. What is the difference between an S Corporation and a C Corporation? S Corporations have the same obligations, powers and protections as C Corporations. The primary difference is how they are taxed. The profits, the losses and the tax attributes of a S Corporation are passed through to the individual stockholders in proportion to their ownership. For example, if the company earns $10,000 in taxable income and has two owners, who each have 50% interest, $5,000 of the profit goes to each owner. The $5,000 is added to each one of their incomes and they are taxed on that amount. The S corporation itself pays no income taxes. The S corporation tax return is an informational return. Whereas a C Corporation is taxed as its own entity. In the above example, the C Corp. would be taxed on the $10,000. at the current corporate tax rates a S corporation has a limited number of stockholders and is limited as

who can be stockholders. You can elect to be taxed as a S Corporation by filing IRS Form 2553. An iCorporation can be either.

8. What is a federal identification number (FEIN) and why do I need one? The FEIN is a specific ID number that is attached to your iCorporation. It is somewhat similar to a social security number for individuals. All companies (not just corporations) that have employees are required to have one. FEIN is used to communicate with the federal government, to file payroll taxes and federal tax returns. You can obtain a FEIN from the federal government by completing a questionnaire at www.IRS.gov.

9. What is a "foreign" Corporation? This is the term a state uses to differentiate a Corporation that is formed in another state from the home state. The foreign Corporation is required to register in any state in which it is "doing business". For example, if a Nevada Corporation wants to qualify to do business in Arizona, it must complete the Arizona registration process and comply with Arizona corporate laws. It must have a resident agent in Arizona.

Don't confuse a "foreign" corporation with an off shore corporation, which is chartered in another country.

10. What name can I use for my Corporation? Your corporate name must be unique to the state in which you register. It cannot be such as to be confused with another Corporation. You apply to the state to obtain the name. States have a reservation process where you can have your name held for a limited period. There is usually a small fee to reserve a name. Your name should include one of the following words: *Corporation, Corp., Incorporated, Inc., Limited, Ltd*, that indicate you are a Corporation.

You need to check with the Secretary of State's website to see if a name is already being used. Most states have rules about certain words in the corporate name. Words like bank, insurance and trust should be avoided unless you are one.

11. What is a nominee? A nominee is a person that is named to take your place as the owner or manager of a corporation you own. For example, on a public list of officers' form, the nominee's name would appear as president, secretary, treasurer and director. You or others may be the stockholders, which are not on public record, and still hold the ultimate control.

12. What is a LLC? LLC are the initials for a Limited Liability Company. This is a fairly new form of business organization that is a hybrid of a regular Corporation and a partnership. The first US recognized LLCs were formed in Wyoming in 1977. They have the advantage of limited liability and separation from it owners (called members), and are taxed like a partnership, where the tax consequences are passed through to the members in proportion to their respective ownership. The same advantage and tax treatment can be obtained by using a S corporation status.

Many pundits of LLCs claim that it is not as formal as a corporation and therefore it is not necessary to maintain as detailed company records or meetings. We suggest that it is just as important to create the formal records for the proper protection. One disadvantage is that it is much harder to maintain confidentially of member/owners, because they are usually listed in public reports. The other disadvantage is there is not a solid body of law firmly established. LLCs do not have hundreds of years of legal precedence to resolve issues like corporations do.

13. What is a non-profit corporation (NPC)? NPCs are usually formed to fund some charitable or philanthropic activity. They are not so different from regular corporations. They operate the same. It has employees and expenses. But, what happens to all the money after the expenses are paid? In a for profit corporation, it is called profit and is owned by the stockholders. Various governmental agencies get a part of the profit in the form of taxes. In a NPC, the left over money is added to surplus funds and it is used to fund the activity for

which it was formed. There are usually no taxes paid, but require tax returns that are extensively detailed as to how the money is used.

Conclusion

Forming an iCorporation is a must if you are in business. Even if you are not in business it may be a good idea. The size of your business does not matter. Big or small, an iCorporation can give you protection and advantages. No other business form gives you the all the advantages of a Corporation, and that is why it is used worldwide to protect, save money, gain privacy, and raise money.

To conform with the latest trends in environmental sensitivity and the "save a tree" movement, we have not added fifty-two pages of fluff and bulk about every individual state's requirements and filing information, I refer the reader to the web site of the state of your interest. Go to www.sos.statename.gov to see their specific information.

All the strategies mentioned in the book are relatively easy and inexpensive to implement. Consult with your advisers to take advantages where you can. We hope the ideas in the book will be useful to you. If we can help, contact us at bdsconsult@gmail.com.

Sample

Vehicle Usage Log

			Odometer			Type	Expenses	
Date	Destination	Business Purpose	Start	Stop	Miles	Type	$Amount	
Totals								

This is the information required by IRS rules

Sample

For discussion only. Seek legal advice before using.

Medical Reimbursement Plan

Medical Care Reimbursement Plan (Plan) of (name of company)

1. Benefits

   The Corporation shall reimburse all eligible employees for expenses incurred by themselves and their dependents, as defined in IRC section 152, as amended, for medical care, as defined in IRC section 213 e, as amended, subject to the conditions and limitations as herein after set forth. It is the intention of the Corporation that the benefits payable to eligible employees hereunder shall be excluded from their gross income pursuant to IRC section 105, as amended.

2. Eligibility

   To be eligible for the plan an employee must:

   -Ordinarily work more than 25 hours per week.

   -Be over the age of 25 years old.

-Ordinarily work more than seven months in the calendar year.

-Has worked for the employer for more than three years.

Those employees covered by a union collective bargaining agreement are not eligible.

The employer may, at its option, cover any and all of the normal non-covered employees noted above.

3. Limitations
   (a) The Corporation shall reimburse any eligible employee no more than $ (dollar amount) in any fiscal year for medical care expenses.
   (b) Reimbursement or payment provided under this plan shall be made by the Corporation only in the event and to the extent that such reimbursements or payment is not provided under any insurance policies, whether owned by the Corporation or the employee, or under any other health or accident or wage continuation plan. In the event that there is such an insurance policy or plan in effect, providing for reimbursement in whole or in part, up to the

extent of the coverage under such policy or plan, the Corporation shall be relieved of any and all liability hereunder.

4. Submission of proof

Any eligible employee applying for reimbursement under this plan shall submit to the Corporation, at least quarterly, all bills for medical care, including premium notices for accident and health insurance, for verification by the Corporation prior to payment. Failure to comply, may at the discretion of the Corporation, terminate such eligible employee's right to said reimbursement.

5. Discontinuation

This plan shall be subject to termination any time by vote of the Board of Directors of the Corporation; provided, however, that the medical care expenses incurred prior to such termination shall be reimbursed or paid in accordance with the terms of this plan.

6. Determination

The President of the Corporation shall determine all questions arising from the administration and interpretation of the plan except for the reimbursement disclaimer of the president. In such case determination shall be made by the Board of Directors.

7. Notification

The secretary will promptly notify all employees covered by the plan and will furnish a copy of the Plan. Acknowledgment of this notification is required from each eligible employee of their acceptance of the plan by a signature.

Adopted by the Board of Directors on (date)

_____, Secretary

Effective Date (   )

Sample. For discussion only. Seek legal advice before using.

Resolution

Minutes of Special Meeting of Directors of (name of company)

A special meeting of the Board of Directors of the Corporation was held on (date), at (time) at the corporate offices.

All of the Directors being present, the meeting was called to order by the Chairman. The Chairman advised that the meeting was called to approve and adopt a medical care expense reimbursement plan. A copy of the Plan was presented to those present in upon motion duly made, seconded and unanimously carried, it was

    Resolved, that the medical care reimbursement plan presented to the meeting is hereby approved and adopted, and a copy of the Plan shall be appended to these minutes, and that the proper officers of the Corporation are hereby authorized to take whatever action is necessary to implement the plan, and it is further

Resolved, that the signing of these minutes by the directors shall constitute full ratification thereof and waiver of notice of the meeting by signatories.

There being no further business to come before the meeting, upon motion duly made, seconded and unanimously carried, the meeting was adjourned.

Secretary_____

Chairman_____

Director_____

Business Startup Checklist

These list items are in rough chronically order. Some will be done simultaneously or be in the process while completing others. Skip any items that do not apply to your type of business.

1. Development a business concept. Write it down on one page.
2. Complete a business plan and a marketing plan to determine how will you get customers/clients.
3. Interview an accountant, attorney or business consultant.
4. Examine needed licenses, permits and state / local regulations for your kind of business.
5. Select a business entity, corporation, LLC, sole proprietorship.
6. Check and secure business name availability, with state and county.
7. Determine your ownership structure.
8. Gather initial startup capital.
9. File your business entity with the state.
10. Do preliminary planning for decisions of the first board meeting.
11. Hold the first board meeting with the ownership.
12. Apply for federal ID number.

13. Apply for S corporation status if appropriate.

14. Prepare a buy/sell agreement with investors, partners and backers.

15. Establish accounting procedures and chart of accounts.

16. Select accounting software or system.

17. Impute all transactions since starting.

18. Solicit investors or obtain financing.

19. Open business bank accounts.

20. Acquire permits and licenses.

21. Select an insurance agent and purchase insurance.

22. Choose a commercial real estate agent.

23. Find appropriate office, retail or production space.

24. Start any space build out or adaptation.

25. Purchase furniture, equipment and fixtures.

26. Select payroll processing or method to do payroll. E filing works best.

27. Interview employee benefits company.

28. Begin interviewing and hiring staff.

29. Start marketing, promotions and advertising.

30. Purchase initial inventory or begin production.

31. Grand opening or introduction to your market.

Additional Resources

1. How to Pay Zero Taxes, by Jeff A. Schnepper

2. Your Income Tax 2013, JK Lasser

3. Loopholes of the Rich, Diana Kennedy, CPA

4. How to be Invisible, by J.J. Luna

5. Lower Your Taxes Big Time, Sandy Botkin, CPA, ESQ.

6. Asset Protection Secrets, by Arnold S. Goldstein, LLM, Phd.

7. A Guide to Asset Protection, by Robert F. Klueger

8. Incorporate Your Business, by Anthony Mancuso, ESQ.

9. Bulletproof Asset Protection, by William S. Reed, JD.

10. IRAs, 401Ks, and other Retirement Plans, Nolo Press.

11. Hide Your Assets and Disappear, by Edmund Pankau

12. How to Do Business with the IRS, by Randy Blaustein, ESQ

13. What the IRS Doesn't Want You to Know, Martin Kaplan, CPA

14. Internal Revenue Code, edited by staff of CCH.

15. IRS.gov. Publication 334 ,Tax Guide for Small Business

16. IRS.gov. Publication 583, Starting a Business and Keeping Records

17. IRS.gov. ID number (EIN's)

Also by Dean Willeford

Cash Out

38 Smart, Quick, Legal Loopholes to Take the Maximun Cash Out of Your Corporation without Disastrous Tax Consequences

"Cash Out" is a gold mine of valuable, no tax or low tax ways to take money out of an owner operated Corporation. In no time you will be applying these strategies to reap huge cash benefits.

Use your own Corporation to get big benefits without the tax headaches.

This book shows entrepreneurs dozens of ways to use big-company loopholes in a small closely owned Corporation. Cash out shows you how to take out over $100,000 per year in cash and benefits and avoid tax pitfalls.

Convert the corporate tax you pay to the IRS to benefits for you and your family.

Learn how to:
- Deduct your vacation.
- Have the IRS pay for your children's allowance and college education.
- Save $10,000 per year in medical and insurance expenses.
- Save over $50,000 per year in deductible retirement plans.
- Get tax-free income for family members.
- Save up to 40% on Social Security and Medicare tax.
- Utilize many other tax breaks

Order on www.Amazon.com. Search CASH OUT.

www.ingramcontent.com/pod-product-compliance
Lightning Source LLC
Chambersburg PA
CBHW072025190526
45166CB00015B/505